"This beautiful book is full of life lessons for children of all ages. The author's bigheartedness and sincerity are evident on every page. Sometimes we can't have what we want, her story tells us, but we can always endeavor to do what is right for others, both people and animals. *Ginger and Moe and the Incredible Coincidence* should be part of every grade school curriculum."

—**JOAN SCHWEIGHARDT**
author of *The Last Wife of Attila the Hun* and other novels

"This book was fun to read. The book showed just how much people really love and care about their cats. I now know what makes people allergic to cats."

—**CHELSEY STRANDSON**
reader from Manchester, New Hampshire, age eight

"This book reaches out to all those pet lovers with allergies, including myself. It is amazing the sacrifices we go through because of the unconditional love we have for our pets. This is a heartwarming story with a feel-good ending that all animal lovers will enjoy."

—**J. LORI KLIMEK**
author of *Jax's Big Adventure* and elementary teacher

GINGER and MOE
and the
Incredible Coincidence

Linda DeFruscio-Robinson

Illustrated by Derita Finchum

BROWN BOOKS KIDS

Ginger and Moe and the Incredible Coincidence

Brown Books Kids
16250 Knoll Trail Drive, Suite 205
Dallas, Texas 75248
www.BrownBooksKids.com
(972) 381-0009

A New Era in Publishing®

ISBN 978-1-61254-935-4
LCCN 2016948183

Printed in the United States
10 9 8 7 6 5 4 3 2 1

For more information or to contact the author, please go to www.GingerAndMoeCatBook.com or www.LindaDeFruscio.com.

Dedication

This book is dedicated with love to my husband, Greg, my sister, Lois (companion to Peaches the cat and Bella and Herbbie the canaries), and my brother, Stephen (companion to Princess the cat).

It is also dedicated to animal lovers everywhere, especially the many people—seniors in nursing homes, college students in dorms, renters in "no pets" zones, and people with allergies, to name a few—who would love to live with animals but can't. Sometimes even the things that are denied us can generate beautiful experiences and happy memories. I hope you find them, as I have.

Ginger and Moe were born in an animal hospital. Their mother gave birth to six kittens, including this brother-and-sister pair. All six kitties got along just fine, but Ginger and Moe had an even deeper bond than the others. They didn't want to be separated. I imagined they would keep each other company if they were left alone. That's why I decided that I would adopt them both.

Ginger and Moe were a mix of Siamese and tiger. Siamese cats have sleek bodies and blue eyes. Tiger cats have some stripes, just like real tigers. You can imagine how beautiful Ginger and Moe were. I couldn't wait to take them home. But the people who ran the animal hospital said they would have to stay with their mother until they were eight weeks old. For young kittens, the first eight weeks are an important time. They learn to socialize and play, are weaned off their mother's milk, and eventually begin eating solid foods.

THE BOSTON
CAT HOSPITAL
THE BOSTON
CAT HOSPITAL

When Ginger and Moe were eight weeks old, I brought a cat carrier to the hospital and picked them up. After a short ride to the house, I opened the cat carrier door and introduced them to their new home.

We began having fun together right away. Ginger and Moe loved to play with me and my husband, Greg. When we were busy with human activities, they loved to play together. Growing up, they chased each other around the house. Sometimes, Ginger hid under the sofa and waited for Moe to pass by so she could stick her paw out and scare him. Sometimes, it was Moe who did the hiding and the scaring. When they were tired, they cuddled together and took naps.

Once a year, I took them to get shots and have their teeth cleaned. They didn't like that, but it was important for them to maintain their good health. As it turned out, it was my health that began to have its ups and downs.

When Ginger and Moe were five years old, I began to have allergies. An allergy is a medical condition that causes someone to become sick after eating, touching, or breathing something that may be harmless to other people. My doctor suggested that I might be allergic to my cats.

"How can that be?" I asked him. "I've had Ginger and Moe for a long time now, and it's only recently that I began to have an allergic reaction."

My allergy doctor explained it this way: Anyone can develop allergy symptoms at any time and at any age. Sometimes people can become allergic to certain chemicals in their pets' dander. Dander refers to the flecks of skin that animals shed. Protein can be found not only in dander but also in a cat's saliva and urine. Some people become allergic to cats because of this.

Cats typically don't like baths, and cats that live indoors, as Ginger and Moe did, don't need them often because they do a good job cleaning themselves. But I wanted to make sure they didn't have excess dander, so I began to bathe them regularly.

Ginger didn't like having a bath. She would cry and meow the whole time she was in the sink. I would cry and meow along with her so she wouldn't feel so bad. Moe didn't like baths either, but he didn't cry or meow. Instead, he scowled, which means he kept a very angry expression on his face. I tried to explain that giving him frequent baths helped temporarily reduce my allergic reactions and symptoms, but he looked angry anyway.

Once they had their baths, I dried them first with a towel and then with a blow-dryer on a very low heat setting. They liked that! Then, I gently brushed their fur, which felt like a massage to them. They liked that too! By the end of their grooming session, they were so relaxed they went right to sleep.

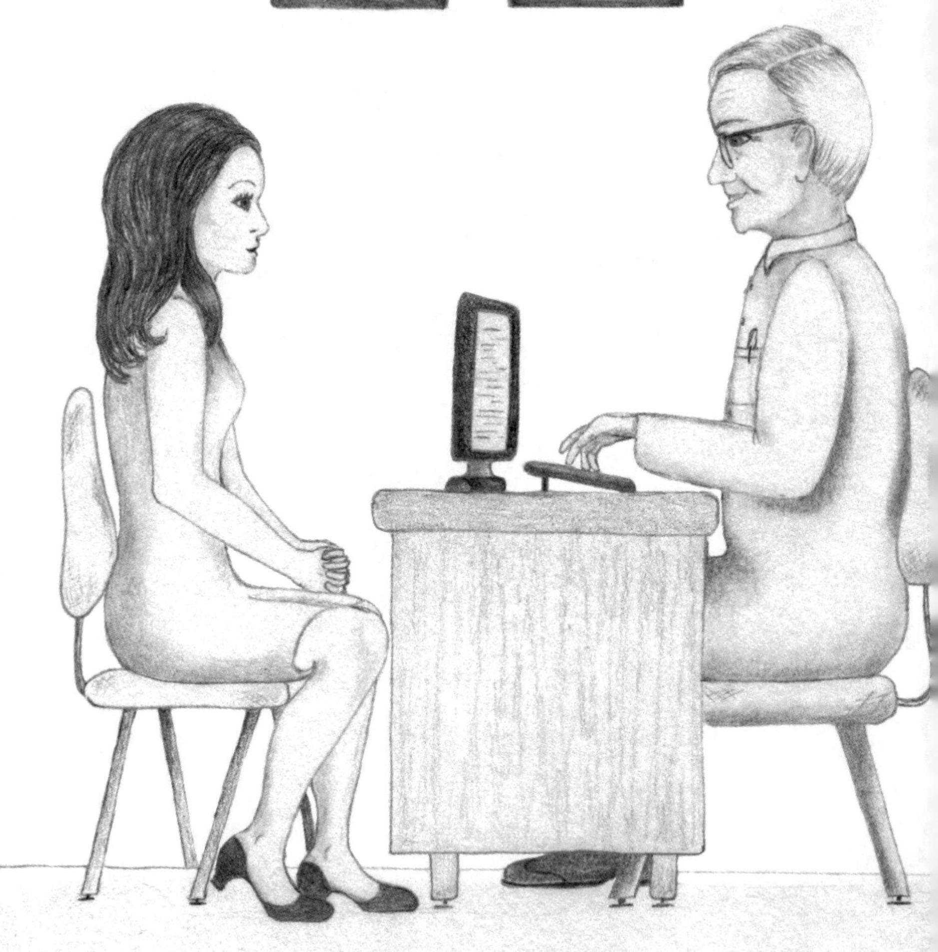

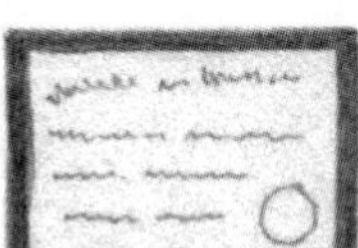

My allergies didn't improve very much over the next five years. My doctor gave me medicines and allergy shots to try to boost my health, but they didn't help me enough. My lung capacity was simply not what it had been before my allergies kicked in. I was having trouble breathing. My doctor advised that I find a new home for Ginger and Moe.

Where would Ginger and Moe go?

I placed an ad in the paper to find a new home for the cats. Many people called and said they would take either Ginger or Moe but not both of them. I told these people that I would not separate them. Some people said they would take both cats, but when I invited them over to meet Ginger and Moe, I didn't think they were quite right.

One woman wanted to adopt Ginger and Moe so that she could

put them to work chasing mice in her barn.

"No," I said. "Ginger and Moe are not working cats."

A man who owned an ice-skating rink wanted to adopt Ginger and Moe to work at his business, chasing rats that came out at night to run back and forth on the cold, cold ice!

"No, no, no," I said.

Many cats are happy to have work controlling rodent infestations, but our cats were not raised that way. And we didn't want them to go to work now, at age ten. We wanted them to have a happy home and lots of love.

After several days of not being able to find a family to take in Ginger and Moe, a nice doctor and his wife, a teacher, called me. They had four daughters, all of whom they homeschooled. They invited me to come to their home and meet their girls. This family wanted Ginger and Moe very badly, not to put them to work but simply to love them. This family was perfect!

I visited Ginger and Moe often after they moved into the doctor's house. I could tell that they were mad at me at first for giving them away. But over time, they adapted to their new environment, and then they weren't so upset with me anymore.

Sometimes, my husband, Greg, came with me when I went to visit them. He liked to get on the floor and play the same games with Ginger and Moe that he had played with them when they lived with us. His favorite game was "horsey." Greg would crawl around on all fours, shaking his head and making funny neighing sounds, just like a horse. Ginger and Moe loved that game. They would run and leap in the air, just the way they did when they were kittens.

Sometimes Greg brought his laser pointer along. Ginger loved it when Greg made the beam of light bounce up and down on the wall. She bounced up and down too, trying to snag that light beam. Lazy Moe didn't bother to chase the beam, but he loved to watch it dance before his lovely blue eyes.

After I said goodbye to Ginger and Moe, I always reminded the doctor and his wife that they must contact me if ever there came a time when they couldn't take care of Ginger and Moe anymore. Ginger and Moe were happy at the doctor's house, but I wasn't so sure they could adjust to anyone else's house. And I was really hoping that maybe my allergies would get better one day.

A year later, the doctor got a call from a humanitarian organization called Doctors Without Borders. They asked him to go to Nicaragua, the largest country in Central America, to work with some people who were sick. He would be taking his whole family with him, and he didn't know how long they would be gone. But they couldn't take Ginger and Moe because there are rules about bringing animals from one country to another. Ginger and Moe would have to be quarantined, which means they would have to be isolated for a long period of time to make sure they didn't carry any infectious diseases. The doctor suggested taking the cats to a shelter.

"No," I said. "Don't take them to a shelter." I knew that many shelters put animals to sleep when no one adopted them. If Ginger and Moe *were* adopted, they might be separated. Greg and I drove right over and picked them up immediately.

At first, Ginger and Moe were very timid back in my house. It was as if they had forgotten about all the love we used to share. But over time, they became affectionate again, and when that happened, I began to cough and sneeze again. Greg and I had an empty shed in the backyard. It was very clean and looked more like a guest cottage than what people usually imagine when you say "shed."

We made a special area in the shed for Ginger and Moe right in front of the biggest window so that they could look out at the birds and the squirrels. But of course we didn't want to leave them alone in the shed all the time. We visited them every day, bringing food and playing with them for a while. Once it got cold, we brought them back inside the house to the heated and finished basement.

Sometimes Ginger and Moe would sit on the edge of the basement steps and watch us do chores in the house. In the evening, when we opened the door to the basement, Ginger and Moe knew it was time to visit or say goodnight. They would quickly dash up the stairs to greet us. They got lots of love as we sat on the steps with them. It seemed they didn't want to wear out their welcome, so they'd run back down the steps after a little while.

I told them, "Oh no, it's okay to come back and visit," and they would run back up with such joy! How smart were these cats? But Greg and I knew that we needed another solution.

My doctor advised me not to have the cats in the bedroom. He also suggested we have no carpets and use washable shades or window treatments. My allergies, however, started up again anyway.

The time had come to find a new owner.

It took a while, but I located a single woman who worked out of her house. Greg and I went to visit her, and we were happy to see that her home was clean, quiet, and safe, a good place for two aging cats. I told her the rules. She must never put Ginger and Moe to sleep, nor could she ever pass them on to another family without my permission. And if the time came when she didn't feel she could take care of them any longer, she must call me at once to come and get them.

I didn't visit Ginger and Moe, because their new owner lived quite far away. But I called now and then to see how the cats were doing. Each time, the woman told me that they were fine, but she thought they missed the activity they had become used to when they'd lived with the doctor and his family.

"Sometimes," she said, "Ginger and Moe look a little sad."

The doctor's daughters missed Ginger and Moe too. They wrote letters telling me about their lives in Nicaragua and asking about the cats. In some of their letters, they admitted that they cried sometimes because they missed Ginger and Moe so much. I admitted that sometimes I cried too. I told them it's okay to be sad, as we can learn lessons about our sadness. Sometimes, life is sad and we just have to deal with it the best we can. We might just understand other people when they are sad too.

But then the story of Ginger and Moe took a surprising turn.

Do you know what a coincidence is? If you are thinking that you should call your grandmother, and, at that moment, the phone rings, and it's your *grandmother* calling *you*, that's a coincidence. Or, if you are wishing for a basketball hoop for your driveway, and then a neighbor knocks on the door and tells you that you may have their basketball hoop because their family is moving and can't take it along with them to the new house, that is a coincidence.

A year after Ginger and Moe moved in with the single woman, she called me to say she had to move to another state and would not be able to bring the cats with her. I was very sad to hear this news. I knew my allergies would start up again, and I also knew that it would be harder than ever to find a good home for Ginger and Moe. People who adopt cats usually want kittens or young cats; not a lot of people want cats who, like Ginger and Moe, were twelve. The veterinarian, however, told me their life expectancy could be many more years because they were healthy indoor cats.

Greg and I drove to the woman's house early the next morning and picked up the cats. We didn't know what we were going to do. Just being in the car with Ginger and Moe got me coughing and sneezing again. We wouldn't even have time to start making calls to try to find them a new home that day because we had a funeral service to attend in the afternoon and a wedding to attend in the evening.

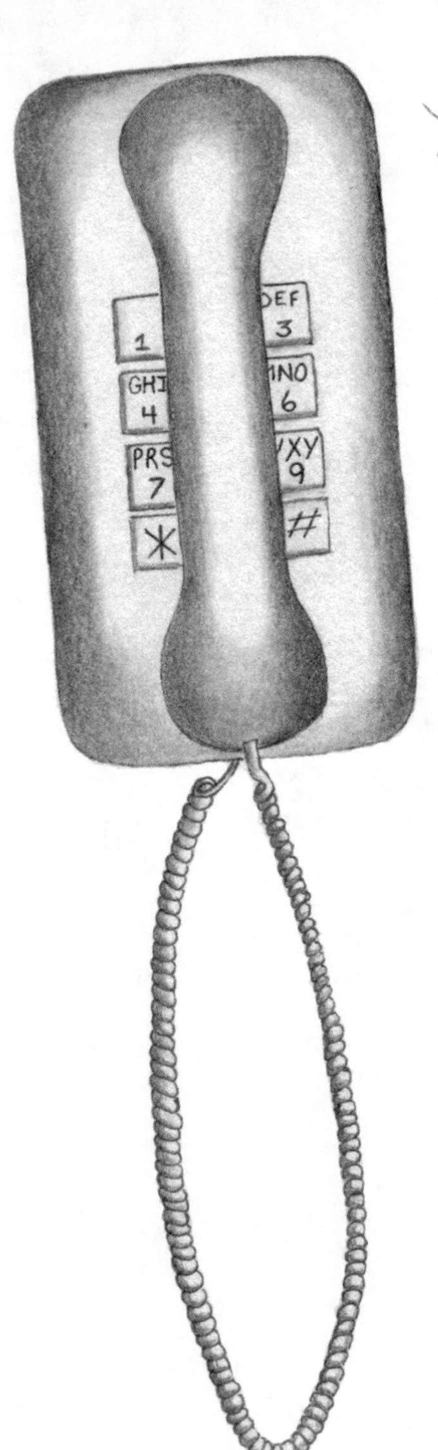

RING

We were just walking in the front door with Ginger and Moe in their cat carrier when the phone rang. I hurried to answer it. It was the doctor, who had just returned with his family from Nicaragua! What a coincidence! They had completed their mission there and would be making their lives in a new house not very far from the one they had lived in before. The doctor said, "My girls cry so much over the cats, and I wish there was a way we could get the woman who has them now to give them up." Little did he know that they were all in for a big surprise!

At first, I was so emotional that I couldn't answer. Then I screamed, "Your wish is granted!" I explained that Greg and I had just picked up Ginger and Moe and they were now back in our house. "Ginger and Moe would love to move back in with you and your family." I added, "I would like to be able to come and visit them like I used to." The doctor said Greg and I would be welcome to visit anytime.

It was one of the happiest days of my life. It was also one of the happiest days in the lives of the doctor's four daughters. And, of course, it was the best day ever for Ginger and Moe.

The Real Ginger and Moe

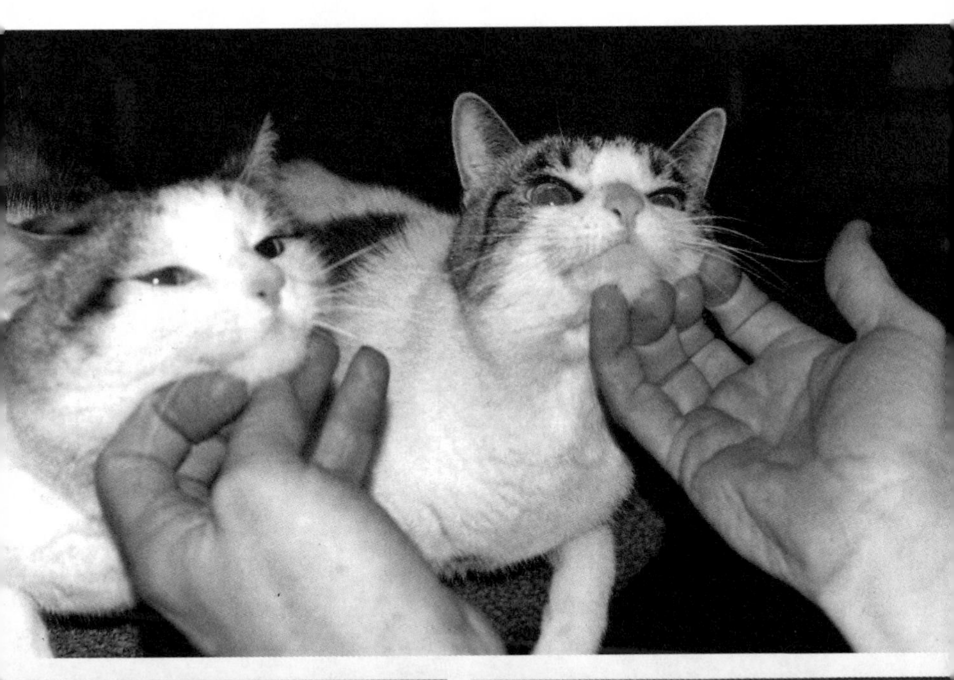

♥Acknowledgments

Thanks to my confidant, mentor, sounding board, soul mate, best friend, and husband, Greg Robinson, for his encouragement and support for all my varied creative endeavors.

Thanks to pharmacist and fellow cat lover Andrew J. Safioleas, my brilliant friend, for reading an earlier draft and offering ideas based on his interactions with children, to whom he teaches violin and piano.

Thanks to animal lover Silka Rothschild for reading an earlier draft as well.

Thanks to my colleague Stephanie Strandson for sharing an earlier draft with her four children, one of whom eagerly offered an endorsement. Stephanie is an animal-rescue volunteer who specializes in nursing abandoned kittens.

Thank you to my talented illustrator, Derita Finchum, for capturing the essence of Ginger and Moe in her drawings.

Thank you to the entire Brown Books Publishing Group professional team for making this book a reality.

I am grateful to my family, friends, co-workers, and clients, whose interest in my writing inspires me daily. Thank you to all.

About The Author

Linda DeFruscio-Robinson is a lifelong author. Her first full-length book, a memoir called *Cornered: Dr. Richard J. Sharpe as I Knew Him*, was published by Twilight Times Books in 2015. *Ginger and Moe and the Incredible Coincidence* is her first children's book. She is currently completing two additional nonfiction titles for adults. Linda is the founder of A & A Laser, Electrolysis & Skin Care Associates Inc. of Newtonville, Massachusetts. She has practiced electrolysis, laser hair removal, and skin care during her thirty-five-year career. Her articles on skin care and hair removal have been published in many national and international journals.

Linda's hobbies, most of which she enjoys with her husband, Greg, include tennis, bowling, long walks, time near the ocean, and quiet time at home, sometimes spent doing sudoku puzzles. The couple has three sons and five grandchildren.

Linda is committed to bringing awareness to young readers' education and to fundraising for medical research. Linda is a supporter of the American Cancer Society, the American Lung Association, and the Multiple System Atrophy Coalition.

Follow your heart and dreams; powerful things may happen.

About The Illustrator

Derita Finchum is a native-born Texan and a natural artist. Her wonderful husband, friends, and family support her long list of artistic pursuits, which include drawing, crafts, sewing, pyrography, and wood-carving. She considers it an honor to illustrate children's books and hopes to pursue it for the rest of her life. Inspired by the support she has received from so many others, Derita uses her talents to encourage others to follow their dreams and to brighten the lives of everyone she can.